The Bernard and Irene Schwartz Series on American Competitiveness

The Case for Wage Insurance

Robert J. LaLonde

CSR NO. 30, SEPTEMBER 2007
COUNCIL ON FOREIGN RELATIONS

Founded in 1921, the Council on Foreign Relations is an independent, national membership organization and a nonpartisan center for scholars dedicated to producing and disseminating ideas so that individual and corporate members, as well as policymakers, journalists, students, and interested citizens in the United States and other countries, can better understand the world and the foreign policy choices facing the United States and other governments. The Council does this by convening meetings; conducting a wide-ranging Studies Program; publishing *Foreign Affairs*, the preeminent journal covering international affairs and U.S. foreign policy; maintaining a diverse membership; sponsoring Independent Task Forces and Special Reports; and providing up-to-date information about the world and U.S. foreign policy on the Council's website, CFR.org.

THE COUNCIL TAKES NO INSTITUTIONAL POSITION ON POLICY ISSUES AND HAS NO AFFILIATION WITH THE U.S. GOVERNMENT. ALL STATEMENTS OF FACT AND EXPRESSIONS OF OPINION CONTAINED IN ITS PUBLICATIONS ARE THE SOLE RESPONSIBILITY OF THE AUTHOR OR AUTHORS.

Council Special Reports (CSRs) are concise policy briefs, produced to provide a rapid response to a developing crisis or contribute to the public's understanding of current policy dilemmas. CSRs are written by individual authors—who may be Council Fellows or acknowledged experts from outside the institution—in consultation with an advisory committee, and are intended to take sixty days or less from inception to publication. The committee serves as a sounding board and provides feedback on a draft report. It usually meets twice—once before a draft is written and once again when there is a draft for review; however, advisory committee members, unlike Task Force members, are not asked to sign off on the report or to otherwise endorse it. Once published, CSRs are posted on the Council's website, CFR.org.

Council Special Reports in the Bernard and Irene Schwartz Series on American Competitiveness explore challenges to the long-term health of the U.S. economy. In a globalizing world, the prosperity of American firms and workers is ever more directly affected by critical government policy choices in areas such as spending, taxation, trade, immigration, and intellectual property rights. The reports in the Bernard and Irene Schwartz series analyze the major issues affecting American economic competitiveness and help policymakers identify the concrete steps they can take to promote it.

For further information about the Council or this Special Report, please write to the Council on Foreign Relations, 58 East 68th Street, New York, NY 10065, or call the Communications office at 212-434-9888. Visit our website, CFR.org.

To submit a letter in response to a Council Special Report for publication on our website, CFR.org, you may send an email to CSReditor@cfr.org. Alternatively, letters may be mailed to us at: Publications Department, Council on Foreign Relations, 58 East 68th Street, New York, NY 10021. Letters should include the writer's name, postal address, and daytime phone number. Letters may be edited for length and clarity, and may be published online. Please do not send attachments. All letters become the property of the Council on Foreign Relations and will not be returned. We regret that, owing to the volume of correspondence, we cannot respond to every letter.

CONTENTS

FOREWORD

The openness of the United States to trade and technological innovation, as well as the flexibility of its labor market, has fueled impressive growth. In such an economy, workers are routinely displaced. Most find new jobs in a reasonable amount of time. But for workers with a long tenure at their previous employer, these new jobs often pay wages much lower than those they earned before. For this group, displacement is much more than a temporary setback.

In *The Case for Wage Insurance*, Robert J. LaLonde recommends rethinking traditional trade adjustment assistance to address this problem. He argues that existing programs, including retraining and unemployment insurance, do too little to help displaced workers whose new jobs pay substantially less than their old ones. Unemployment insurance, for example, makes up for lost income during unemployment but not for reduced income after reemployment. To fill this gap, Professor LaLonde proposes to shift resources from existing programs to a displacement insurance plan—effectively, a generous earnings supplement for a number of years—for workers facing a long-term reduction in wages.

Ultimately, well-designed displacement insurance could ease long-tenured workers' fears of job and income loss, thereby diminishing opposition to free trade and other policies perceived as at fault. In this way, it could help Americans continue to enjoy the benefits of trade and openness, and help the United States maintain its competitiveness and leadership in the global economy.

This Council Special Report was produced by the Council's Maurice R. Greenberg Center for Geoeconomic Studies as part of the Bernard and Irene Schwartz Series on American Competitiveness. The Council and the center are grateful to the Bernard and Irene Schwartz Foundation for its support of this important project.

Richard N. Haass
President
Council on Foreign Relations
July 2007

ACKNOWLEDGMENTS

I am grateful to the members of the Council Special Report advisory committee that met twice to provide comments on an outline and early drafts of this report. Members of the advisory committee include: Katherine Baicker, Anne Board, Emily S. DeRocco, Thomas R. Donahue, Louis Gerber, Owen E. Herrnstadt, Dalmer D. Hoskins, Lori G. Kletzer, Robert E. Litan, William D. Novelli, Shaun O'Brien, Michael J. Piore, Patricia Ruggles, Gordon S. Wayne, and John N. Yochelson. Special thanks are due to Patricia Ruggles for agreeing to chair the committee.

I also would like to thank Douglas Holtz-Eakin for encouraging me to write this report. Council President Richard N. Haass and Director of Studies Gary Samore commented on the drafts. Chad Waryas coordinated the efforts of the many parties who assisted in the publication and dissemination of this report. Dalmer D. Hoskins offered early and insightful advice. Sebastian Mallaby, who succeeded Douglas Holtz-Eakin as director of the Council's Geoeconomic Center, contributed the final edit.

Finally, I must acknowledge Louis S. Jacobson, Daniel G. Sullivan, and Robert H. Topel, with whom I have had many conversations about this topic over nearly two decades. Besides our research, these conversations have had an enormous influence on my thinking about the consequences of worker displacement. All errors and omissions are mine.

Robert J. LaLonde

EXECUTIVE SUMMARY

An important component of U.S. productivity growth and economic competitiveness is a flexible labor market that shifts workers quickly into the jobs where they are most needed. Much of the time, this job shifting is fairly painless: Workers quickly find new positions that pay at least as much as their previous ones, often without an intervening spell of unemployment. But prime-aged and older workers can sometimes suffer large, long-term income losses. Such workers' well-founded fears about job displacement lead them and their advocates to resist policies such as free trade that are sometimes blamed for job loss. This resistance harms the majority of households because trade helps to lower prices, raise real incomes, and promote economic growth. It also has foreign policy consequences since it threatens the United States' ability to play its traditional post–World War II role as the bulwark of a relatively open international trading system. And by reducing the dynamism of the U.S. economy, resistance to trade and other pro-growth policies can weaken the nation's long-term ability to exert global leadership.

This Council Special Report documents the causes, risks, and consequences of worker displacement. It describes the services currently available to displaced workers, and contends that most of these services do not address the risks faced by prime-aged and older workers, even when they are cost-effective and appropriately designed for less vulnerable members of the workforce. Current policies emphasize unemployment insurance, which is appropriate if the main cost of job loss is temporarily lower income while unemployed. But for many long-tenured displaced workers, the greatest costs of job loss are lower wages following reemployment. Existing policies do not address this long-term reduction in income.

This report recommends that policymakers aid prime-aged and older workers who get rehired at lower wages by providing them with an earnings supplement. This "displacement insurance" pays benefits to eligible workers only after they find new jobs and only if their new earnings are less than their old ones. When targeted at those who face the largest and most persistent long-term losses from losing a job, displacement insurance can begin to address the substantial risks that many prime-aged and older workers confront in a dynamic economy.

There is broad consensus among labor policy experts on the necessary characteristics of displacement insurance. By limiting benefits to 50 percent of the difference between pre- and post-displacement earnings, most displacement insurance proposals provide incentives for displaced workers to search for more productive jobs at higher wages, reducing the moral hazard inherent in any insurance program. Further, most proposals do not discriminate between displaced workers by making the insurance conditional upon being from a declining industry or geographic area or on being from a trade-affected industry or firm; nor are conditions attached to age or the duration of joblessness. Displacement is not limited to workers in a particular sector or region of the country or age group, the argument goes, so there is no reason to exclude some big-earnings losers while including others.

The shortcoming of these standard displacement insurance proposals is that they fail to provide adequate coverage to many prime-aged displaced workers who experience permanent and severe income losses. Most displacement insurance proposals cap benefits at around $10,000 per year, limit the duration of benefits to two years, and exclude workers earning above $50,000 per year. These program characteristics would exclude many middle-aged, middle-class displaced workers who experience the largest wage and income losses as a result of job loss. But even with these workers excluded, the standard insurance proposals nonetheless cost $3 billion to $4 billion per year, financed with a monthly tax or "insurance premium" of approximately $2 to $3 per worker.

Unfortunately, to displaced workers experiencing substantially reduced lifetime earnings as a result of displacement, a two-year earnings supplement provides limited comfort. To aid vulnerable prime-aged workers, displacement insurance should provide benefits that extend beyond two years. But such extensions require either workers or their employers to pay higher premiums, or policymakers to divert substantial resources from other programs.

If proposed displacement insurance premiums were doubled, policymakers likely could provide benefits for four years following job loss. That would be enough to provide meaningful coverage against permanent earnings losses for workers who are nearing the end of their working lives. But such an extension would still cover only a small portion of the losses experienced by some prime-aged displaced workers who anticipated working for another fifteen to twenty years prior to losing their jobs.

In principle, a more comprehensive displacement insurance program could be financed by further raising premiums paid by either workers or their employers. But policymakers also should consider diverting resources from other labor market programs. As explained in this report, existing retraining initiatives offer a false promise of meaningful aid. Resources currently earmarked for retraining could be used to help finance displacement insurance, thereby giving displaced workers the choice of using their benefits to supplement their incomes or to pay for training programs if that is their preference.

Alternatively, policymakers could finance displacement insurance by diverting resources from the existing unemployment insurance program. This approach amounts to changing the emphasis of the safety net from solely insuring against relatively small temporary earnings losses for many workers toward providing insurance against extremely large permanent earnings losses experienced by relatively few workers. One way to change the emphasis incrementally is to extend the waiting period before unemployment insurance claimants start to receive benefits.

To be sure, all the foregoing options for financing displacement insurance are controversial. But this report contends that there are compelling rationales for each one. By extending the benefit period of existing displacement insurance proposals, they would assuage many prime-aged and older workers' well-founded fears of job displacement. In so doing, they would bolster the political consensus in favor of flexible labor markets, consolidating American competitiveness and the nation's ability to sustain its leadership around the world.

COUNCIL SPECIAL REPORT

INTRODUCTION

Productivity growth is central to the competitiveness of the U.S. economy. More productive workers give firms the flexibility to sell products at lower prices in world markets, raise product quality, pay higher wages, and attract international capital. Since the mid-1990s, U.S. business sector productivity has grown at an annual rate of more than 2.5 percent, markedly faster than the rate during the previous two decades.

Discussions about the drivers of productivity growth in the United States tend to highlight new computing and communications technologies or the competitive pressures from openness to international trade. But a cornerstone of U.S. productivity growth is a flexible labor market that moves workers between jobs. This flexibility is evidenced by the rapid pace of domestic job creation and destruction. In many industries, approximately 15 to 25 percent of jobs are either created or destroyed annually and, economy-wide, approximately 10 percent of all jobs are eliminated. The continuous elimination of jobs and the creation of new ones have the effect of moving workers into the positions where they are most needed. This labor market dynamism is an essential complement to trade and technological innovation: as production methods evolve rapidly thanks to technological changes and the spur of international competition, the deployment of the nation's human capital has to shift in order for productivity gains to be realized. Labor market flexibility is thus a central contributor to U.S. economic growth, living standards, and international competitiveness.

The economy-wide benefits from the process of job creation and destruction exceed the losses experienced by those who are forced to change jobs. Most displaced workers find new jobs that pay at least as much as their previous positions, and everyone gains from lower prices and better-quality products. However, some prime-aged and older workers are permanently harmed by this otherwise beneficial feature of the U.S. economy. For these workers, job loss is associated with large, long-term income losses. These workers' well-founded fears of job displacement lead them to resist policies that promote economic growth and American competitiveness. To foster U.S. economic success, policymakers should design measures that address this anxiety. Displacement insurance that pays displaced workers an earnings supplement when they are reemployed at lower pay represents one strategy for aiding the group most adversely affected by job loss—long-tenured displaced workers.

The idea of coupling economic change and openness with compensation for losers has a long pedigree. According to trade historian I. M. Destler, the trade adjustment assistance program, or TAA, was first suggested in a Council on Foreign Relations paper prepared during World War II. TAA gained broad exposure when it was proposed to the Eisenhower administration by the leader of the United Steelworkers union. The Trade Expansion Act of 1962 included limited measures to assist workers adversely affected by trade, which helped to persuade major labor unions to support the bill's passage. In the same year, Congress enacted the Manpower Development and Training Act, which initially was designed to retrain workers who had lost jobs as a result of technological change and "automation" of their workplaces. Only later, during the long economic expansion of the 1960s, did these programs start to focus on the economically disadvantaged as part of the war on poverty.

The landmark Trade Act of 1974, which created the Office of the U.S. Trade Representative, boosted TAA, providing trade-affected workers up to one year of income supplements. Starting in the 1980s and especially during the 1990s, Congress substantially expanded support for retraining programs targeted specifically at permanent job losers. These workers were not economically disadvantaged and often had well-established work histories prior to being displaced not only from their jobs but often also from their industries.

Harkening back to this tradition of assisting those who lose as a result of economic change and expanded trade, Congress substantially expanded TAA with the passage of the Trade Act of 2002. The act provided a tax credit for health insurance and expanded eligibility to agricultural workers, secondary workers, and workers displaced as a result of the outsourcing of production to a country party to a trade agreement with the United States. Further, the program included, for the first time, a pilot wage insurance scheme, as well as increased funding for job searches, relocation services, and worker retraining programs. The program is due to expire at the end of September 2007, and Senate and House leaders are currently debating further expansion.

Trade adjustment assistance and retraining programs have proved disappointing, however, both in their impacts on displaced workers and in their ability to make trade deals more politically viable. That is partly because these programs have been modestly funded. Even after the expansion enacted in 2002, annual spending on trade adjustment assistance amounts to less than $1 billion a year, while spending on retraining for displaced workers under the Workforce Investment Act of 1998 amounts to somewhat more than $1 billion per year—extremely small sums given that U.S. gains from trade are estimated at up to $1 trillion annually. The wage insurance component of trade adjustment assistance is likewise limited because it is restricted to workers over fifty, and anybody earning over $50,000 is excluded from the program.

At the same time, the linking of displacement assistance to trade has helped foster the false impression that displacement largely results from liberalized trade, whereas the truth is that technological progress and changing patterns of consumer demand contribute more to job churning. A program that might have made trade deals more politically salable has therefore risked having the opposite effect of cementing the connection in popular debates between trade and economic hardship. The misleading connection between assistance and trade has also created an undesirable double standard: workers displaced by trade are offered help while those displaced for other reasons often are not, even though there is little policy justification for this distinction and it can be hard to tell what caused a particular worker to lose his or her job.

Congress needs to address this problem by going beyond the traditional conception of trade adjustment assistance and modestly funded low-intensity retraining programs for displaced workers. Policies toward displaced workers need to be better funded than in the past. They need to include all displaced workers rather than just those affected by trade, and they need to offer meaningful wage insurance. In principle, these prescriptions could have bipartisan appeal. Wage insurance extends help to middle-aged, middle-class workers, which should attract support from labor unions and their allies. But wage insurance proposals envision paying benefits only when eligible displaced workers find and keep jobs, which should make the program palatable to conservatives.

Unfortunately, until recently, both labor groups and conservatives have been skeptical of wage insurance, characterizing it alternatively as "burial insurance" or as excessively expensive. But there have been hopeful signs recently in Congress. Senator Max Baucus (D-MT), the chairman of the Senate Finance Committee, which has jurisdiction over trade, and Senator Norm Coleman (R-MN) are pushing a TAA proposal that includes wage insurance. Jim McDermott, a Democratic representative from Washington State and chairman of the Joint Economic Committee, and Senator Charles Schumer (D-NY) have coauthored a freestanding wage insurance bill. House Republicans have offered an alternative wage insurance plan that would be funded at the expense of unemployment insurance. None of these proposals is sufficiently ambitious, as this paper will argue. But they are evidence of the hopeful gathering of support for the concept of wage insurance.

The politics of trade have grown so toxic that wage insurance cannot guarantee a resumption of liberalization. But polling evidence suggests it would help. Kenneth F. Scheve and Matthew J. Slaughter, the leading experts on globalization and public opinion, report that Americans understand that trade brings lower prices and greater variety, but that a growing majority nonetheless opposes trade liberalization because of fears of stagnant or falling wages. Similarly, a Program on International Policy Attitudes (PIPA)–Knowledge Networks Poll conducted in January 2005, "Americans on Globalization, Trade, and Farm Subsidies," concludes that, "If the government would make substantial, visible efforts to mitigate the side effects of expanded trade, support for the growth of trade would be substantially higher than it is. When the possibility of helping workers adapt to changes associated with increased trade is considered, support for free trade becomes very strong."

Moreover, irrespective of the potential benefits from trade liberalization or from technological changes that lead to permanent job losses, wage insurance is desirable in its own right. As this report explains, wage loss following displacement can be as financially catastrophic as the loss of a house. But whereas private markets offer insurance for storms and fire, no such insurance is available when a middle-aged worker loses a job and suffers a permanent drop in wages. There is a market failure here, and government should correct it.

Displaced workers are those permanently laid off as a result of economic conditions adversely affecting their employer. These workers lose their jobs not because of their performance but because of shifts in consumer demand, technological advances, expanded international trade, government policy changes, natural disasters, or idiosyncratic factors affecting businesses.

Statistics from the U.S. Bureau of the Census Displaced Workers Surveys indicate that approximately 4 percent of U.S. workers are displaced every two years. These job losses usually entail a period of temporary unemployment before workers find new jobs that pay at least as much as their previous ones. Most displaced workers are unemployed for less than six months, and a substantial share are unemployed for less than five weeks. Policymakers have designed programs to make these bouts of unemployment brief and relatively painless: reemployment services aid workers' transition from one job to the next; unemployment insurance protects workers against temporary loss of income. But the consequences of job loss can be severe for those who have worked for a long time with their pre-displacement employer. Most do find new jobs, but they must accept significant pay cuts.

When researchers compare earnings losses among otherwise similar workers, the shortfall between pre- and post-displacement wages tends to rise with tenure. Figure 1 shows data for workers displaced between 1999 and 2001: workers who had more than twenty years of job tenure experienced wage losses that were about 30 percentage points greater than those experienced by counterparts with less than one year of tenure. Wage losses for workers with between four and ten years of tenure averaged about 5 percent, though the wage shortfall for this group has been as much as twice as large in other periods. By contrast, studies consistently find that workers displaced from jobs lasting less than three years generally experience little if any significant reduction in wages after they are reemployed.

**Figure 1: Percentage Difference Between Wages Post- and Pre-Displacement,
by Tenure with Pre-Displacement Employer**

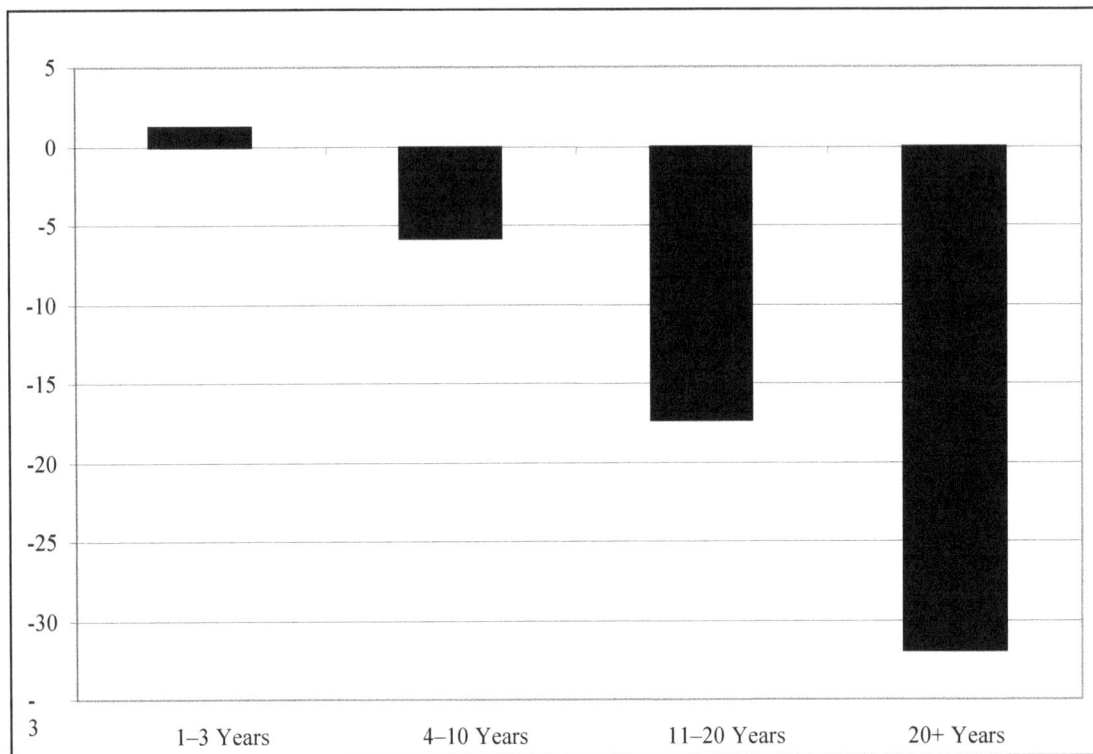

Source: Author's calculations using Henry Farber (2004), Table 3, page 24, based on calculations from the *U.S. Bureau of the Census 2002 Displaced Worker Survey.*

Recognizing that workers who accumulate significant tenure prior to displacement constitute an important part of the workforce, the U.S. Department of Labor has for two decades tracked their fortunes. It defines long-tenured workers as those with three or more years of service. This group constitutes approximately one-third of all displaced workers.

Although the Department of Labor's threshold of three years of tenure includes many workers who experience small long-term losses after displacement, during the past two decades a significant fraction has experienced large drops in income. As shown in Figure 2, the weekly wages of approximately one-fourth to one-third of these workers (some 250,000 annually) have been more than 20 percent below their weekly wages prior to displacement. One study found that Pennsylvania workers with six or more years of tenure who lost their jobs in the 1980s as part of mass layoffs or plant closings were earning about 25 percent less six or more years after being displaced. Displaced workers who changed industries experienced especially severe losses, but earnings losses were still substantial among displaced workers who found new jobs in the same industries.

Figure 2: Percentage of Long-Tenured Displaced Workers with Earnings Losses Greater Than 20 Percent

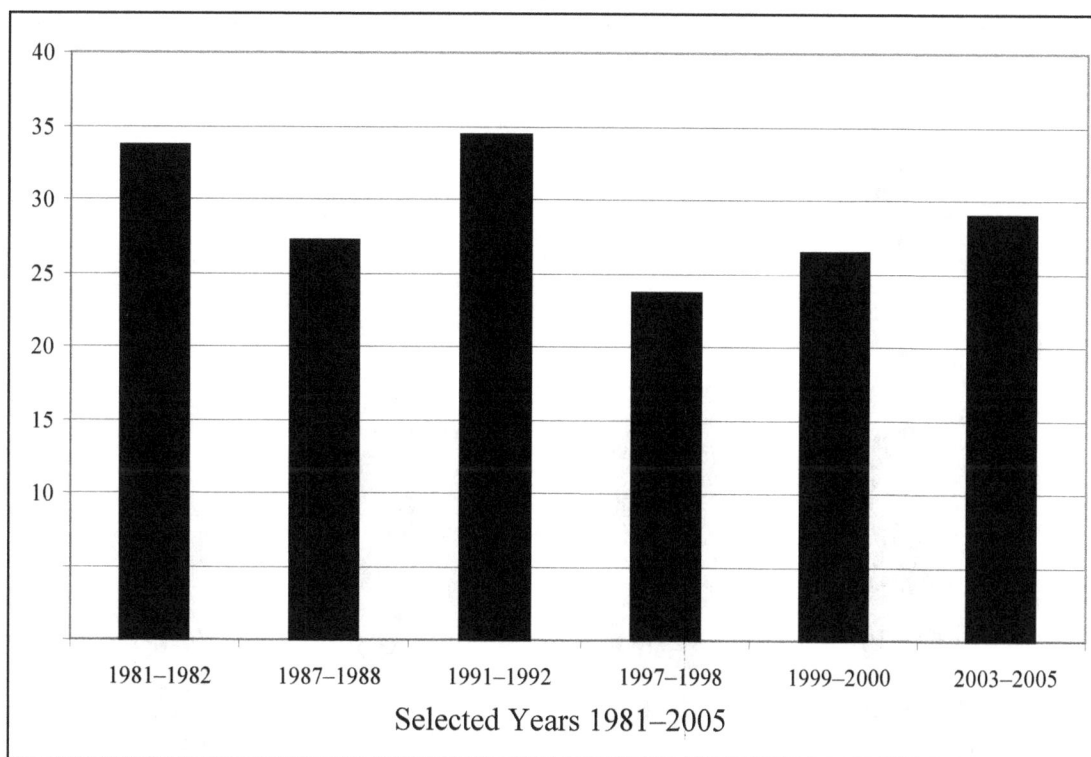

Source: Author's calculations using Henry Farber (2004), Table 3, page 24, based on calculations from the *U.S. Bureau of the Census 2002 Displaced Worker Survey.*

Statistics from the Department of Labor's Displaced Worker Surveys indicate that the likelihood of such a costly job loss is substantial compared to other costly events in a person's life. During the past two decades and over two business cycles that included unusually long economic expansions, *two-year* displacement rates of long-tenured workers ranged between 2.5 to 4 percent. That means companies displace approximately one in fifty to one in eighty of their long-tenured workers each year. About half of these displacements result from a mass layoff or a plant closing.

Fortunately for prime-aged and older workers, job tenure is also associated with a lower probability of job loss. As shown in Figure 3, in 1999 and 2000 the two-year displacement rate among workers with up to three years of tenure was 5.3 percent.

Among workers with three to four years of tenure, the displacement rate was 3.2 percent. And for workers with ten or more years of tenure, the displacement rate was 1.9 percent. To some degree, job tenure confers seniority and protects workers from a costly job loss.

Figure 3: Percentage of Workers Displaced by Years of Job Tenure Between 1999–2000

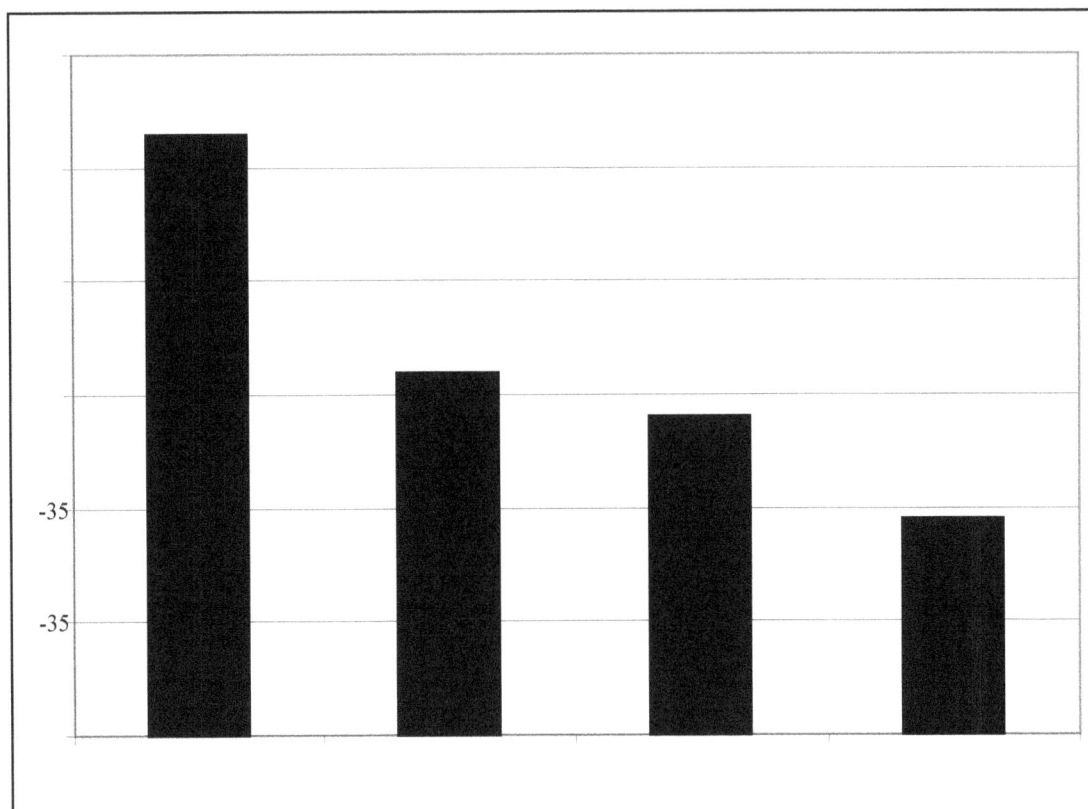

Source: *Monthly Labor Review*, June 2004.

Much discussion of the plight of displaced workers has focused on workers in trade-affected manufacturing industries. But workers across the economy face the risk of displacement. Figure 4 shows that the two-year displacement rate is highest among manufacturing workers, at 4.7 percent, but it is 2.5 percent in the services sector and exceeds 3 percent in the wholesale and retail trade sectors. When workers in nontraded sectors are displaced, their long-term earnings losses are often substantial. These data show that the traditional approach to adjustment assistance, which is to limit it to workers who can demonstrate that they have been displaced by trade, is misconceived. Focusing on trade-affected workers is not an effective way to target those most harmed by costly displacements.

10

**Figure 4: Two-Year Displacement Rates for Long-Tenured Workers
by Selected Major Industries Between 1999–2000**

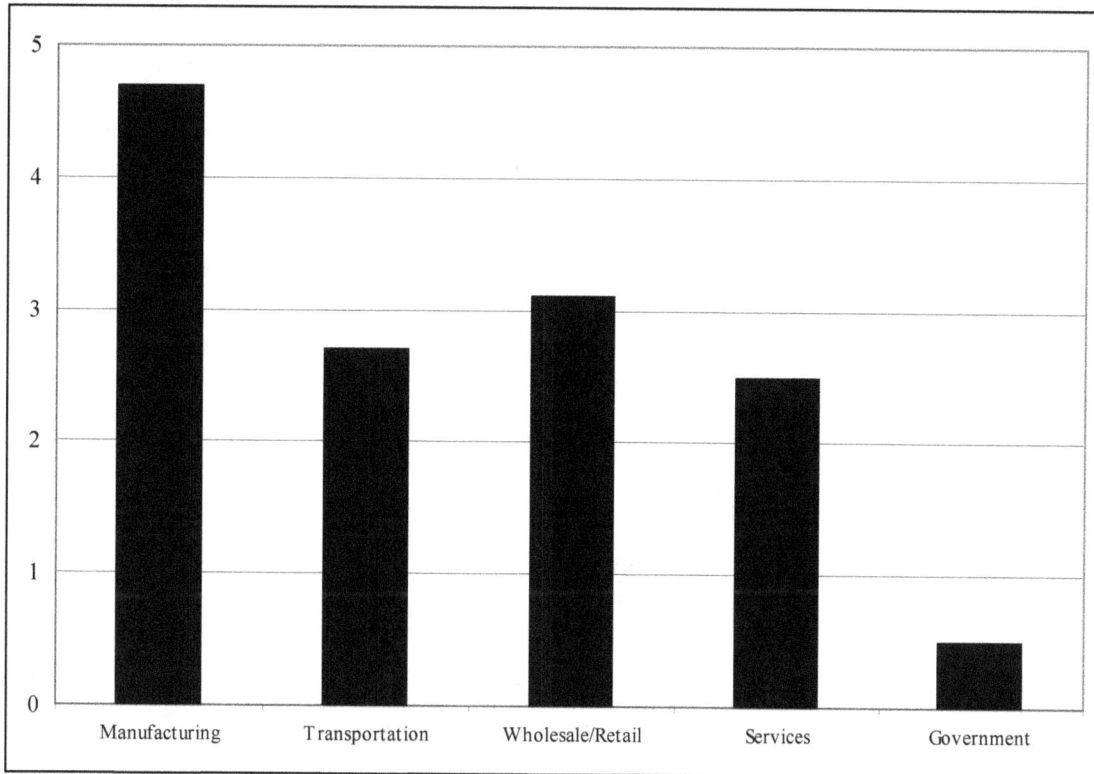

Source: *Monthly Labor Review*, June 2004.

An Example of the Lifetime Costs of Displacement

To understand the potential consequences of job loss for long-tenured workers, consider a forty-year-old, male high-school graduate who had accumulated six years of tenure and earned $40,000 annually before being displaced by his employer. Once he is displaced, skills he acquired with his former employer may be of little or no value to other employers. Moreover, if his old company compensated him partly on the basis of seniority, he will lose this advantage upon joining another company. So although the worker can find a new job relatively quickly, a job might pay only $30,000, or 25 percent less than his pre-displacement job. Studies indicate that a forty-year-old man will work, on average, an additional twenty years before leaving the labor force. If the 25 percent pay cut persists, the present value of this man's losses over the rest of his working life will amount to about $165,000.[1] Even this amount understates the worker's total losses because it does not include the value of foregone pension and health benefits or reduced employer contributions to Social Security.

It is clear that the cost of wage loss, which the government does not currently insure, can dwarf the cost of job loss, for which the government does provide coverage. Suppose our forty-year-old displaced worker was unemployed for twenty weeks before finding a new job, which is longer than we would expect. He would experience a loss of about $5,000, net his unemployment insurance benefits—a loss that amounts to about 3 percent of his earnings reduction once reemployed. The $165,000 impact of long-term wage loss is more aptly compared to the loss of a home, since home prices averaged about $160,000 across the United States in 2000. But whereas home insurance is widely available, job insurance is not. No wonder long-tenured workers who perceive their jobs to be at risk are so fearful of the economic policies that they blame for this risk.

Two further points are worth noting. First, the consequences of displacement do not necessarily get worse as workers age. A sixty-year-old man is likely to work for about six more years; in order for displacement to be as costly for him as for the forty-year-old, his wage drop would have to be roughly three times larger. Because a 75 percent wage drop is exceedingly unlikely, policies that target services to the oldest displaced workers are not targeting those most likely to be the hardest hit by displacement. For this reason, the current wage insurance program, which limits benefits to workers aged fifty and older, is missing some of the most important potential beneficiaries.

Second, studies that compare the consequences of displacement across countries indicate that the structure of the labor market and labor market institutions play a role in determining the costs of worker displacement. Reemployment earnings losses are larger in countries such as the United States, Canada, and the United Kingdom. These countries have greater earnings inequality and relatively high returns to skills. By contrast, reemployment earnings losses are smaller in continental European countries, which have smaller wage differences between high- and low-skilled workers. As a result, when displaced workers find new jobs, it is more likely that their pay will be closer to that of

---

[1] This calculation discounts the future earnings losses at a rate of 2 percent, the approximate real interest rate.

their previous jobs. This suggests that the case for wage insurance is strongest in the Anglo-Saxon economies.

THE CASE FOR AIDING LONG-TENURED DISPLACED WORKERS

There are two main arguments for providing assistance to long-tenured displaced workers. First, such aid helps to allay workers' fear of displacement and, as a result, may reduce resistance to policies conducive to economic growth. Second, government policy in this area responds to the failure of private markets to provide insurance that protects workers from the risk of costly displacement. A possible third argument is that, although studies suggest that technological change and shifts in consumer demand are the most common causes of displacement, government should soften the consequences of displacement because its own policies contribute to it. Trade liberalization, growth promoting economic polices, or even well-designed environmental standards that benefit most in our society can also have large adverse effects on some workers. When government policy causes workers to lose their jobs, it is appropriate to consider redistributing some of the gains associated with these policies to those who are harmed by them.

MARKET FAILURE AND WAGE INSURANCE

For long-tenured workers, job loss is potentially as costly as a serious automobile accident, having one's house burn down, or becoming permanently disabled. Moreover, costly displacement appears to be more likely to occur than these other dramatic events in a person's life. The statistics cited above from the Displaced Worker Surveys suggest that each year, long-tenured workers have between a three-tenths and one-half of 1 percent chance of losing their jobs and experiencing long-term annual earnings losses of 20 percent or more. Unlike costly displacement, however, insurance is available to protect against these other risks. Some displacement insurance is provided privately through the practice in larger firms of making severance payments to laid-off employees that rise with years of service. But severance benefits are available to only a small percentage of

14

long-tenured displaced workers, and their availability is not tied to a measure of the wage loss experienced by the worker.

The absence of a strong private market for displacement insurance is understandable. Such insurance is difficult to provide profitably. The variation in risks and costs of displacement among workers becomes a problem when workers who are most likely to buy displacement insurance are the ones who expect displacement to affect them the most severely. Because of this adverse selection, any private insurer that enters this market is likely to find itself underwriting the most costly risks.

CAN EXISTING POLICIES AID DISPLACED WORKERS?

Policymakers have implemented several strategies to aid displaced workers after they lose a job. These measures have been controversial, and many critics have labeled them "burial insurance." Critics argue that rather than focusing on workers only after their jobs have ended, policy should focus on upgrading skills to make job loss less likely in the first place. Suggested strategies include lifelong learning initiatives, flexible education accounts, subsidized worker retraining in establishments vulnerable to mass layoffs or closings, and requiring, as some countries do, that employers spend a share of their wage bill each year on training.

These alternatives deserve consideration to the extent that they help workers to become more productive in their current jobs, to find better-paying jobs, and even to fare better when displaced. But to believe that policies should primarily be designed to reduce the incidence of displacement presumes that the dynamic process of job creation and destruction is a form of market failure that can be fixed through appropriate policy. Although misguided fiscal and monetary policies can cause excess job creation and destruction, overall this process is an asset to the economy rather than a liability.

The better approach is to avoid strategies designed to reduce the likelihood of job loss, and instead to pursue policies that cushion it. Existing policies that address the unique circumstances of displaced workers focus on incentives to return to work, retraining programs, and limited experiments with wage subsidies following reemployment. A shortcoming that they all share is that they do not provide much aid to long-tenured displaced workers.

Reemployment Services

Reemployment services help displaced workers to reassess their skills, learn about the range of employers that require such skills, and find new jobs. Evaluations indicate that such services are cost-effective, but by design these services cannot mitigate displaced workers' long-term earnings losses because they focus on getting displaced workers employed quickly in the best job possible. They do not address the problem that the best job possible likely pays displaced workers less than their previous jobs.

The benefits of reemployment programs are small relative to displaced workers' total earnings losses. These programs, when they work, rarely shorten the duration of unemployment by more than two weeks. Further, the gains in earnings from rapid reemployment are often partially offset by losses of unemployment insurance benefits. For example, two weeks of employment for the forty-year-old displaced worker increases his earnings by about $1,150; at the same time, he loses $770 in unemployment insurance benefits, and he also pays more taxes. In the end, reemployment services increase his income, but this gain should hardly mollify his concern about job loss.

Another implication of this assessment of reemployment policies is that the Worker Adjustment and Retraining Notification Act (WARN) that requires employers to provide sixty days' advance notice of a mass layoff or plant closing only marginally improves outcomes. At best, this policy amounts to two months of severance pay, which is only a fraction of displaced workers' expected reemployment earnings losses. Getting a leg up on a job search just will not make that much difference to their long-term incomes. The majority of long-tenured displaced workers in the United States find jobs relatively quickly, so trying to stem earnings losses while unemployed does little to mitigate the long-term losses that they experience when reemployed.

Training has more potential to aid displaced workers than reemployment services because it is designed to boost skills, productivity, and hence long-term wages. In the private sector, skilled workers also acquire more on-the-job training. An initial investment in training can create a virtuous circle.

There are, however, difficulties with relying on retraining to aid long-tenured displaced workers. Substantial investments in training are necessary in order to mitigate a significant portion of displaced workers' long-term earnings losses. Past public sector investments in training have been small, so policymakers have no experience with ambitious retraining efforts. And even if older displaced workers are able to acquire new skills as efficiently as younger persons, it is still the case that their incentives to participate in retraining are less, as are the benefits society receives from their retraining.

To understand the shortcomings of retraining initiatives, it is helpful to think of investments in worker retraining like an investment in the stock market. If the real rate of return on investments in worker retraining were 10 percent per year, it would beat historical rates of return in the stock market and would also be larger than estimates of the rate of return from children's formal schooling. Once we begin analyzing investments in workers' skills from this viewpoint, we can realistically assess the likely effects of retraining on displaced workers' earnings.

Studies of training initiatives for displaced workers indicate that government subsidies for training generally amount to a few thousand dollars per displaced worker; rarely does a worker receive as much as $10,000 worth of retraining. Workers' investment of time and effort must be factored in, too: $10,000 worth of retraining requires nine months of course work and delays a worker's return to work. If the forty-year-old displaced worker considered above could have earned $30,000 annually, the direct and the (prorated) indirect costs of retraining come to a total investment in retraining of about $32,500.

What gain in annual earnings is reasonable to expect from a $32,500 investment in retraining? If we assume a rate of return of 10 percent, the forty-year-old displaced worker's earnings would increase by $3,800 per year for the rest of his working life.

Notice that despite these upper-end estimates, the earnings increase still falls far short of the $10,000 annual loss expected from displacement. If we double the investment to $20,000 in direct costs and two academic years of full-time retraining, the projected effects on earnings would still not offset this displaced worker's earnings loss. Such a training investment approximates that made by a displaced worker who returns full-time to a community college to receive two years of vocational retraining.

Our calculations indicate that past failures of government retraining initiatives to offset a significant fraction of displaced workers' losses cannot be blamed on poor implementation. Even if retraining programs were implemented by the finest operators in the nation, $10,000 or $20,000 investments are simply too small to offset the reemployment earnings gap. Current retraining initiatives under the Workforce Investment Act (WIA) or trade adjustment assistance programs, which generally involve far smaller investments per worker, amount to a false promise for long-tenured displaced workers and cannot be expected to quell their fears of costly displacements.[2]

---

[2] Established as part of the Trade Act of 1974, the trade adjustment assistance (TAA) program provides employment and training services and up to fifty-two weeks of unemployment compensation to workers who either lost their jobs or experienced lower earnings as a result of increased imports.

WHY DISPLACEMENT INSURANCE MIGHT HELP

Existing policies do not provide much aid to long-tenured displaced workers because they fail to address the most costly risk of job loss. Reemployment programs that shorten unemployment by a few weeks or cost-effective training programs that raise annual earnings by about $1,000 annually do not address the potential for large reemployment earnings reductions. If policymakers want to aid the group most harmed by displacement, their policies must focus less on job loss and more on earnings loss. Although displacement insurance is part of the 2002 trade adjustment assistance program, there is relatively little experience with this strategy.[3]

Displacement insurance aids displaced workers who are paid substantially less on their new jobs than they were paid on their prior jobs. Most displacement insurance proposals recommend using the unemployment insurance system to pay long-tenured displaced workers an earnings supplement after they are reemployed. The benefits paid equal a percentage, often proposed to be 50 percent, of the difference between displaced workers' pay in their old jobs and their pay in their new jobs. Most proposals also cap payments at a maximum, often $10,000 per year, and limit the duration of benefits to two years. The rationale for capping displacement insurance payments is that more educated, better-paid displaced workers, at least until recently, appeared to fare better after losing their jobs than their less educated counterparts who were likely to be paid less to begin with. Therefore, this cap ensures that displacement insurance is targeted at middle- and lower-income workers most likely to experience persistent earnings losses following displacement. Finally, displacement insurance proposals usually call for limiting benefits to reemployed displaced workers earning less than $50,000 or some other earnings threshold.

---

[3] In August 2003, policymakers launched the Alternative TAA program to serve older TAA-eligible workers for whom retraining is not likely to be appropriate. In addition to reemployment services, Alternative TAA participants receive an earnings supplement that offsets 50 percent of the shortfall between their pre- and post-displacement earnings up to a maximum benefit of $10,000 paid over a period of two years. Alternative TAA participants who earn more than $50,000 annually are ineligible to receive this earnings supplement.

If a goal of displacement insurance is to lessen the well-founded fears that long-tenured workers have about job loss, such earnings thresholds, if set too low, undermine an important part of the program. The rationale underlying wage insurance is to aid those who experience the largest losses from displacement. The poor or even the working poor usually will not be among this group. Workers who earned low wages prior to losing their jobs are unlikely to experience large wage losses once they are unemployed. Instead, wage insurance programs are most important to middle-aged, middle-class workers who risk larger wage losses following their displacements. Setting earnings thresholds too low undermines the objective of wage insurance because it potentially excludes many of these workers. Wage insurance is not an antipoverty program; instead it addresses a substantial market failure that affects middle-aged, middle-class workers and their willingness to embrace beneficial economic policies.

A reason why displacement insurance proposals cover only 50 percent as opposed to 100 percent of workers' reemployment earnings losses is that at 100 percent coverage, reemployed workers have less incentive to continue searching for better-paying jobs. Only new jobs that pay more than their pre-displacement jobs would be worth seeking. But the economy would still benefit if these workers sought better-paying jobs, even if they did not pay as much as their old jobs. If displacement insurance covered 100 percent of workers' earnings losses, much productive "on-the-job" employment search would cease.

Another rationale for the underlying characteristics of displacement insurance proposals is to keep program costs low. This objective is especially apparent in proposals that limit the duration of reemployment benefits to two years. This time limit markedly lowers these proposals' costs. But the two-year time limit also substantially undercuts the most compelling aspect of using an earnings supplement to provide displacement insurance. The promise of a two-year earnings supplement provides little insurance to middle-aged, long-tenured workers who experience substantial long-term earnings losses after displacement. In the case of the forty-year-old displaced worker, displacement insurance with a two-year limit would offset only about an additional 5 percent of the present value of his earnings loss. Unless long-tenured workers are close to retirement, such proposals do not insure against much of their expected losses. To address the needs of prime-aged, long-tenured displaced workers, an effective displacement insurance program must last longer than two years.

Most displacement insurance proposals recommend that any job loser who experiences reemployment losses should be eligible to receive an earnings supplement. These proposals usually reject using other eligibility criteria such as evidence that the displaced worker was from a declining industry, occupation, or geographic area, a trade-affected industry or firm, their ages at displacement, or the duration of their joblessness. Because these losses are not limited to workers in a sector or region of the country or age group per se, there is no reason to exclude some big-earnings losers but to include others in a displacement insurance program. To displaced workers facing an uncertain future of lower earnings, it does not matter which event beyond their control caused them to lose their jobs.

In addition to tying displacement insurance to reemployment earnings losses, it is sensible to limit eligibility to long-tenured workers—say, those workers who have worked for twelve or more quarters with their primary pre-displacement employer. As discussed above, pre-displacement job tenure is a good predictor of longer-term reemployment earnings losses; the longer the tenure, the more likely it is that workers will have skills that cannot be transferred to another firm. So workers with little prior tenure would not be eligible to receive displacement insurance payments because, even if their new jobs pay less, it is not likely that their income losses will last for long. Existing proposals that advocate paying wage insurance benefits to workers with as little as one year of pre-displacement tenure are not targeting the largest wage losers or those experiencing the most pronounced obsolescence of their skills. They risk providing benefits that constitute a windfall to workers who only briefly held a high-paying job.

Some labor policy experts contend that displacement insurance can be provided in the form of a reemployment bonus that pays workers a lump sum if they return to work quickly. Such bonuses provide greater incentives to search for work both before and after displacement. Because recipients receive no additional benefits beyond the bonus after they are reemployed, they also have greater incentives to engage in a job search than they would with an earnings supplement.

Although attractive in theory, reemployment bonuses have been disappointing in practice. They do not have large effects on the rate at which people return to work. And such bonuses are an exceedingly blunt form of insurance. For this reason, an earnings supplement has an advantage over a bonus.

Earnings Supplements and the Forty-Year-Old Worker

To understand how an earnings supplement might affect displaced workers' incomes and offset some of their earnings losses, let us return to the forty-year-old high-school educated male who earned $40,000 on his previous job, but cannot find a new job that pays more than $30,000. The benefit of wage insurance to this worker starts with the fact that he will find a job faster. All workers who receive unemployment insurance benefits experience reduced incentives to return to work, but this is especially true of long-tenured workers because the benefits are large relative to their prospective earnings. Whereas unemployment benefits usually equal roughly 50 percent of workers' pre-displacement pay, for the forty-year-old displaced worker these benefits represent approximately 75 percent of likely post-displacement earnings. That means that so long as he is still eligible to receive unemployment insurance benefits, the incentive to work is low—only $4.80 per hour before taxes. Add wage insurance into the picture and the incentive to work rises by 50 percent, to $7.20 per hour. As a result, studies estimate that displacement insurance proposals will shorten the duration of insured unemployment spells by two to three weeks. So if we assume the forty-year-old in our example is unemployed for fifteen weeks following job loss if no wage insurance is available, the availability of insurance would cut that period to twelve weeks. In both cases, we assume that our forty-year-old worker receives unemployment compensation after a one-week waiting period.

Let us start by considering the forty-year-old displaced worker's income under current policy. As shown in Table 1, during the first six months following his job loss, he receives $5,385 in unemployment insurance benefits and $6,346 in earnings. His total income during the period is $11,731, or $8,269 less than his income had he not been displaced. Over the entire two-year period following displacement, his income losses total $23,270. Beyond this point, we assume that the displaced worker remains employed—an optimistic assumption—and that his losses amount to $10,000 annually.

Table 1: Effects of Wage Insurance on Long-Tenured Displaced Workers

	Earnings	Earnings if Displaced			Earnings under Standard Displacement Insurance Proposals		
Months		Earnings	Benefits	Income	Earnings	Benefits	Income
0–6	20,000	6,346	5,385	11,731	8,077	5,577	13,654
6–12	20,000	15,000	0	15,000	15,000	2,500	17,500
12–18	20,000	15,000	0	15,000	15,000	2,500	17,500
18–24	20,000	15,000	0	15,000	15,000	2,500	17,500
2-Year Totals	80,000	51,346	5,384	56,730	53,077	13,077	66,154
3–4 Year Totals	80,000	60,000	0	60,000	60,000	0	60,000

Source: Author's calculations based on the experience of a forty-year-old displaced worker who earned $40,000 annually prior to displacement and $30,000 upon reemployment. Calculations assume the worker is unemployed for fifteen weeks if no displacement insurance is available, and twelve weeks if displacement insurance is available. Unemployment insurance replaces 50 percent of pre-displacement earnings while unemployed after a one-week waiting period. Displacement insurance in the form of an earnings supplement pays 50 percent of the difference between the worker's pre- and post-displacement earnings for up to two years from the time he filed a valid claim for unemployment insurance. Earnings refer to self-employment or wage and salary earnings; benefits refer to unemployment insurance and displacement insurance benefits; income is the sum of earnings and benefits.

How would existing displacement insurance proposals aid this unemployed worker? As shown in Table 1, during the first six months following his job loss, he receives $5,577 in unemployment insurance benefits and earnings supplements, and $8,077 in earnings. His total income during the period is $13,654, or $6,346 less than what he would have earned had he not been permanently displaced. Over the entire two-year period following displacement, his income losses would total $13,346. During the first two years after being displaced, these losses are 40 percent less than losses that he would experience under current policy. Most of the reduction results from $8,846[4] in

---

[4] Author's calculations assume unemployment benefits of $384.64 per week. Under the wage insurance program, displaced workers are unemployed for twelve weeks and receive benefits of $4,231.05 over eleven weeks, after a one-week waiting period following displacement. The remaining $1,346 in benefits represents the earnings supplement paid to the worker following reemployment in week twelve. Between months six and twenty-four, the worker receives an additional $7,500 in wage insurance benefits, or $2,500 every six months. Together, the worker receives $8,846 in earnings supplement over this two year period.

earnings supplements benefits. Because most proposals limit the duration of displacement insurance to two years, in subsequent years his losses amount to $10,000 annually, as they do under current policy.

How Much Would Displacement Insurance Cost?

Studies estimate that a displacement insurance program similar to the proposal outlined above would cost $3 billion to $4 billion per year, or about 10 percent of annual unemployment insurance benefit payments. This estimate includes the cost of a tax credit that eligible displaced workers could use to purchase health insurance. A more appropriate program that adequately addresses the risk of large permanent earnings losses would cost more. For example, a program offering four years of insurance would be roughly double the cost of a two-year program. But even a four-year program would offset only about 12 percent of the present value of the forty-year-old displaced worker's lost earnings.

One way to provide extended benefits to some displaced workers without increasing proposed expenditures is to impose a modest "deductible" on reemployment earnings losses. This change would mean that fewer long-tenured workers would receive displacement insurance benefits, but they would be better targeted toward those hardest hit by job loss. For example, a displacement insurance program would pay out benefits when reemployment earnings losses exceeded 5 percent of pre-displacement pay. A rationale for such a deductible is that policymakers should cover the larger losses that would be the most difficult for displaced workers to self-insure and leave workers to cover the smaller losses on their own.

An enhanced displacement insurance program could also be financed by a monthly tax or "insurance premium" of approximately $2 to $3 per worker. This premium could be added to existing unemployment insurance taxes paid by employers on behalf of their employees or it could be paid directly by employees. An advantage of the latter option is that, as with other kinds of insurance, it provides a rationale for allowing workers' displacement insurance benefits to be free from income taxes.

In addition to increased unemployment insurance taxes, policymakers could also shift resources from existing programs targeted at displaced workers to a displacement insurance program. Studies have yet to make a compelling case as to why resources for long-tenured displaced workers should be specifically earmarked for retraining. In any case, diverting training resources to finance displacement insurance would not necessarily limit displaced workers' training options. If they wished, displaced workers could use their earnings supplements to acquire training through their local community or technical colleges. These institutions are already heavily subsidized by state and local governments. Besides providing displaced workers with more options, this approach also would improve current policy, which ties receipt of training to remaining unemployed.[5]

Yet another source of revenue for a displacement insurance program could come from existing unemployment insurance. Policymakers could extend the waiting period for benefits from one or two weeks to three or four weeks. The most recent program statistics suggest that a two-week increase in the waiting period would make about $4 billion available annually, enough to finance a two-year displacement insurance program.[6] Extending the current waiting period would modestly shift the focus of the unemployment insurance program away from providing compensation for relatively temporary and small income losses toward the more costly reemployment earnings losses.

If policymakers choose this option to help fund a wage insurance program, unemployed workers would have to self-insure against smaller income losses, but in return would receive more protection against the risk of a largely uninsurable costly displacement. A two-week increase in the waiting period would increase these unemployment insurance-eligible workers' income losses on average by about $550. Government should consider allowing or perhaps even requiring workers in jobs covered

---

[5] Some commentators have criticized the alternative TAA program, because it requires workers to forgo training in order to receive displacement insurance benefits. Although in principle this criticism has merit, in practice program participants can use their benefits to pay tuition for schooling and retraining offered at local community and technical colleges or at private organizations.

[6] Statistics from the U.S. Department of Labor Employment and Training Administration indicate that the average weekly UI benefit is $275. During 2006, about seven million beneficiaries received at least one week of benefits. An increase in the waiting period by one week would reduce total benefit payments by about $1.9 billion.

by unemployment insurance to maintain individual retirement accounts (IRAs) for this purpose.

Finally, although existing proposals envision a national wage insurance program, states could launch wage insurance systems on their own. Of course, Congress may have to help by amending federal law to give states the option of using resources from the present unemployment insurance system or from the trade adjustment assistance or Workforce Investment Act programs to pay for wage insurance. That would allow for a series of wage insurance programs with different policy parameters rather than a single national wage insurance program. Such regional variation would mirror the decentralization that already exists in unemployment insurance.

CONCLUSION

Job loss is a common experience for U.S workers and has many causes. Although studies indicate that the volatile process of job creation and destruction promotes growth and higher living standards, for some prime-aged and older workers, job loss has costly long-term consequences. Not all displaced workers share this risk and indeed, most do not. But many long-tenured displaced workers may never find new jobs that pay as well as their previous ones. The risk of a costly displacement is highest for prime-aged workers in their forties and fifties who have many years left in their working lives, not for older workers close to retirement.

Existing policy consists of well-targeted services for the typical displaced worker for whom most of the cost of losing a job is lower earnings while unemployed. But for many long-tenured workers, the primary cost of displacement is lower wages on their new jobs. Existing policy does not address this cost of job loss. Unemployment insurance addresses the temporary earnings losses of most displaced workers. But as a system of insurance, it has the peculiar feature that it expects workers to self-insure against job losses that lead to large long-term declines in earnings, and instead insures against relatively small, temporary earnings losses. Likewise, resources available for retraining allow for too small an investment in new skills to mitigate long-tenured displaced workers' earnings losses significantly. Promises cannot be expected to persuade at-risk, prime-aged workers that they will be protected in a rapidly changing economy.

The current safety net is analogous to automobile insurance that refuses to pay out when cars are totaled, but generously covers for fender benders. Given a choice, consumers would prefer insurance to work the other way around—witness the spread of high-deductible policies. It may seem harsh to compare typical spells of unemployment to a fender bender; unemployment is stressful to individuals and their families. But it is important for policymakers to recognize the substantial difference between the consequences of job loss for most of the unemployed and the effects of wage loss for some long-tenured displaced workers. For at least a part of the workforce, the fear of calamitous long-term wage loss is justified, and it is understandable that advocates should push hard for polices that reduce the risk of such events, even if these policies slow beneficial changes to the economy. To be effective in assuaging workers' fears of costly displacement, the duration of these earnings supplements needs to be extended well beyond the two-year period recommended in most current proposals.

As Congress debates trade adjustment assistance and grapples with globalization, it is important to remember what is at stake here. Over the past two decades, the openness of the United States to trade and technological innovation has fueled the nation's growth and underpinned its global leadership; but that same openness has simultaneously eroded public support for the policies that make growth possible. Between 1975 and 2005, as technological change proceeded quickly and U.S. imports as a share of gross domestic product (GDP) more than doubled, the bipartisan pro-trade consensus fell apart: whereas the trade acts of 1962 and 1974 passed Congress by overwhelming margins, President Bill Clinton failed to secure "fast-track" trade negotiating authority from Congress in the 1990s, and President George W. Bush secured the approval of the House of Representatives for the renamed Trade Promotion Authority in 2001 by just one vote. There are good reasons for these changing views: trade and technological change do inflict losses on some groups, and the losers cannot be expected to like this. Unless something is done to help mature workers who face the risk of severe wage losses, their advocates will continue to frustrate trade deals and otherwise raise barriers to growth.

This paper has considered the various options for assisting displaced workers. Proposals aimed at dampening labor market flexibility are ill-conceived because such churn is on balance an economic asset. Proposals to invest in retraining overestimate how much difference conventional training initiatives can make. Even the standard proposals for wage insurance are flawed, because they are too limited to assuage the well-founded anxiety of mature workers about the consequences of losing their jobs. Given the shortcomings of these various options, a more ambitious experiment with wage insurance is a policy risk worth taking. It could be financed by collecting a modest premium from workers or by shifting resources from less useful programs; it could be implemented centrally or on a state-by-state basis. The onus is on those who dislike this proposal to come up with a more plausible way to underpin public support for a dynamic economy.

REFERENCES

Aaronson, Stephanie, Bruce Fallick, Andrew Figura, Jonathan Pingle, and William Wascher. "The Recent Decline in Labor Force Participation and its Implications for Potential Labor Supply." Board of Governors of the Federal Reserve System, 2006.

Brainard, Lael, Robert Litan, and Nicholas Warren. "Insuring America's Workers in a New Era of Offshoring." *The Brookings Institution,* Policy Brief No.143 (2005).

Ciecka, James E., and Gary R Skoog. "The Markov (Increment-Decremenet) Model of Labor Force Activity: Extended Tables of Central Tendency, Variation, and Probability Intervals." *Journal of Legal Economics*, Vol. 11 (2001), p. 23.

Ciecka, James E., and Gary R. Skoog. "The Markov (Increment-Decremenet) Model of Labor Force Activity: New Results Beyond Work-Life Expectancies." *Journal of Legal Economics,* Vol. 11 (2001), p. 1.

Corson, Walter, Paul Decker, Phillip Gleason, and Walter Nicholson. "International Trade and Worker Dislocation: Evaluation of the Trade Adjustment Assistance Program." Final Report: DOL Contract No: 99-9-0805-75-071-01 (Princeton: Mathematica Policy Research Inc., 1993).

Davidson, Carl, and Stephen A. Woodbury. "Wage-Rate Subsidies for Dislocated Workers." *Upjohn Institute Staff* Working Paper No. 95-31, (January 1995).

Davis, Steven J., John C. Haltiwanger, and Scott Schuh. *Job Creation and Destruction.* Cambridge, MA: MIT Press, 1996.

Davis, Stephen J., and John C. Haltiwanger. "Gross Job Flows." In Orley Ashenfelter and David Card, eds., *Handbook of Labor Economics*, Vol. 3B. Amsterdam, New York, and Oxford: Elsevier Science, North Holland, 1999, pp. 2711–2805.

Decker, Paul T., and Walter Corson. "International Trade and Worker Displacement: Evaluation of the Trade Adjustment Assistance Program." *Industrial and Labor Relations Review* Vol. 48 (1995), pp. 758–74.

Decker, Paul T., and Christopher J. O'Leary. "Evaluating Pooled Evidence from the Reemployment Bonus Experiments." *Upjohn Institute Staff* Working Paper, 1994.

Farber, Henry. "The Incidence and Costs of Job Loss: 1982–1991." *Brookings Papers on Economic Activity: Microeconomics.* Vol. 1 (1999), pp. 73–119.

Farber, Henry. "Job Loss in the United States 1981–2001." Princeton University, Industrial Relation Section Working Paper No. 471, May 2003.

Farber, Henry. "What Do We Know about Job Loss in the United States?: Evidence from the Displaced Worker Survey, 1984–2004." *Economic Perspectives* XXIX (2). Federal Reserve Bank of Chicago, pp. 13–22.

Freeman, Richard. "Trade Wars: The Exaggerated Impact of Trade in Economic Debate." National Bureau of Economic Research Working Paper No. 10000 (September 2003).

Heckman, James J., Robert J. LaLonde, and Jeffrey Smith. "The Economics and Econometrics of Active Labor Market Programs," in Orley Ashenfelter and David Card, eds., *Handbook of Labor Economics*, Vol. 3A. Amsterdam: North Holland, 1999, pp. 1865–2097.

Heckman, James J., Lance Lochner, and Ricardo Cossa. "Learning-By-Doing vs. On-the-Job Training: Using Variation Induced by The EITC to Distinguish Between Models of Skill Formation." *National Bureau of Economic Research*, No. 9083 (July 2002).

Heckman, James J., Lance Lochner, and Petra Todd. "Fifty Years of Mincer Earnings Regressions." Unpublished working paper, University of Chicago, March 2003.

Helwig, Ryan. "Worker Displacement in 1999–2000." *Monthly Labor Review* (June 2004), pp. 54–68.

Juhn, Chinhui, Kevin M. Murphy, and Robert H. Topel. "Current Unemployment, Historically Contemplated. *Brookings Papers on Economic Activity,* Vol. 1 (2002), pp. 79–116.

Jacobson, Louis, Robert LaLonde, and Daniel Sullivan. *The Costs of Worker Dislocation.* Kalamazoo, MI: W. E. Upjohn Institute for Employment Research, 1993.

Jacobson, Louis, Robert J. LaLonde, and Daniel Sullivan. "Earnings Losses of Displaced Workers.*" American Economic Review* (1993), pp. 685–709.

Jacobson, Louis, Robert J. LaLonde, and Daniel Sullivan. "Is Retraining Displaced Workers a Good Investment?" *Economic Perspectives* XXIX (2) (2005), pp. 47–66.

Jacobson, Louis, Robert J. LaLonde, and Daniel Sullivan. "Long-term Earnings Losses of High-Seniority Displaced Workers." *Economic Perspectives* XVII (6) (1993), pp. 2–20.

Jacobson, Louis, Robert J. Lalonde, and Daniel Sullivan. "The Impact of Community College Retraining on Older Displaced Workers: Should We Teach Old Dogs New Tricks?" *Industrial and Labor Relations Review*, Vol. 58 (2005), pp. 398–415.

Jacobson, Louis, Robert J. LaLonde, and Daniel Sullivan. "The Returns from Classroom Training for Displaced Workers." *Journal of Econometrics* Vol. 125 (2005) pp. 271-304.

Kane, Thomas, and Cecila Rouse. "The Community College: Educating Students at the Margin Between College and Work." *Journal of Economic Perspectives*, Vol. 13 (Winter 1999), pp. 63–84.

Kletzer, Lori G. "Job Displacement." *Journal of Economic Perspectives,* Vol. 12 (1998), pp. 115–36.

Kletzer, Lori G. "Trade and Job Loss in U.S. Manufacturing, 1979–94." In Robert C. Feenstra, ed., *The Impact of International Trade on Wages*. Chicago: University of Chicago Press, 2000, pp. 349–93.

Kletzer, Lori G. "Trade-related Job Loss and Wage Insurance: A Synthetic Review." *Review of International Economics*, Vol. 12 (2004), pp. 724–48.

Kletzer, Lori G., and Robert E. Litan. "A Prescription to Relieve Worker Anxiety." *Institute for International Economics Policy Brief*, PB01-2 (2001).

Knudsen, Eric I., James J. Heckman, Judy L. Cameron, and Jack P. Shonkoff. "Economic, Neurobiological, and Behavioral Perspectives on Building America's Future Workforce." *PNAS* 103 (2006), pp. 0155-10162.

Kuhn, Peter. *International Perspectives on Worker Displacement*. Kalamazoo, MI: W.E. Upjohn Institute for Employment Research, 2002.

LaLonde, Robert J. "The Promise of U.S. Employment and Training Programs." *Journal of Economic Perspectives*, Vol. 9 (1995), pp. 149–168.

LaLonde, Robert J. "Employment and Training Programs." In Martin Feldstein and R. Moffitt, eds., *Tested Transfer Programs in the United States*. Chicago: University of Chicago Press, 2002.

Leigh, Duane E. *Does Training Work for Displaced Workers? A Survey of Existing Evidence*. Kalamazoo, MI: W.E. Upjohn Institute for Employment Research, 1990.

Mukoyama, Toshihiko, and Aul Ayseg Sahin. "Why Did the Average Duration of Unemployment Become So Much Longer?" Department of Economics, Concordia University and CIREQ, Federal Reserve Bank of New York, 2004.

Neal, Derek. "Industry-specific Capital: Evidence from Displaced Workers." *Journal of Labor Economics,* Vol. 13 (October 1995), pp. 653–77.

Parsons, Donald, and Shuaizhang Feng. "Insuring Displaced Workers: Human Capital Losses and Severance Pay Design." Mimeo, George Washington University, December 2004.

Ruhm, Christopher. "Are Workers Permanently Scarred by Job Displacements?" *American Economic Review*, No. 81 (1991), pp. 319–23.

ABOUT THE AUTHOR

Robert J. LaLonde is a professor in the Harris School of Public Policy at the University of Chicago. Professor LaLonde first joined the University of Chicago in 1985, where he taught for ten years at the Graduate School of Business and the Harris School. From 1995 to 1998, Professor LaLonde served as an associate professor of economics at Michigan State University. He has been a research fellow at the National Bureau of Economic Research since 1986, served as a senior staff economist at the Council of Economic Advisers during the 1987–88 academic year, and was the deputy director of the Northwestern University–University of Chicago Joint Center for Poverty Research. He currently serves as a faculty affiliate with the University of Chicago's Center for Human Potential and Public Policy.

His research focuses on six areas: program evaluation; education and training of the workforce; economic impacts of immigration on developed countries; the costs of worker displacement; the impact of unions and collective bargaining in the United States; and the consequences of incarceration on labor market and social welfare outcomes. Professor LaLonde received his PhD in economics from Princeton University.

ADVISORY COMMITTEE FOR
THE CASE FOR WAGE INSURANCE

Katherine Baicker
COUNCIL OF ECONOMIC ADVISERS

Anne Board
MCKINSEY & COMPANY, INC.

Emily S. DeRocco
DEPARTMENT OF LABOR

Thomas R. Donahue
WORK IN AMERICA INSTITUTE

Louis Gerber
COMMUNICATIONS WORKERS OF
AMERICA, AFL-CIO

Owen E. Herrnstadt
INTL. ASSN. OF MACHINISTS AND
AEROSPACE WORKERS

Dalmer D. Hoskins
INTERNATIONAL SOCIAL SECURITY
ASSOCIATION

Lori G. Kletzer
UNIVERSITY OF CALIFORNIA,
SANTA CRUZ

Robert E. Litan
EWING MARION KAUFFMAN
FOUNDATION

William D. Novelli
AARP

Shaun O'Brien
AARP

Michael J. Piore
MASSACHUSETTS INSTITUTE OF
TECHNOLOGY

Patricia Ruggles
NATIONAL ACADEMY OF SCIENCES

Gordon Wayne
DEPARTMENT OF LABOR

John N. Yochelson
BUILDING ENGINEERING AND
SCIENCE TALENT

Note: Council Special Reports reflect the judgments and recommendations of the author(s). They do not necessarily represent the views of members of the advisory committee, whose involvement in no way should be interpreted as an endorsement of the report by either themselves or the organizations with which they are affiliated.

MISSION STATEMENT OF THE MAURICE R. GREENBERG CENTER FOR GEOECONOMIC STUDIES

Founded in 2000, the Maurice R. Greenberg Center for Geoeconomic Studies at the Council on Foreign Relations works to promote a better understanding among policymakers, academic specialists, and the interested public of how economic and political forces interact to influence world affairs. Globalization is fast erasing the boundaries that have traditionally separated economics from foreign policy and national security issues. The growing integration of national economies is increasingly constraining the policy options that government leaders can consider, while government decisions are shaping the pace and course of global economic interactions. It is essential that policymakers and the public have access to rigorous analysis from an independent, nonpartisan source so that they can better comprehend our interconnected world and the foreign policy choices facing the United States and other governments.

The center pursues its aims through:

- Research carried out by Council fellows and adjunct fellows of outstanding merit and expertise in economics and foreign policy, disseminated through books, articles, and other mass media;

- Meetings in New York, Washington, DC, and other select American cities where the world's most important economic policymakers and scholars address critical issues in a discussion or debate format, all involving direct interaction with Council members;

- Sponsorship of roundtables and Independent Task Forces whose aims are to inform and help to set the public foreign-policy agenda in areas in which an economic component is integral;

- Training of the next generation of policymakers, who will require fluency in the workings of markets as well as the mechanics of international relations.

COUNCIL SPECIAL REPORTS
SPONSORED BY THE COUNCIL ON FOREIGN RELATIONS

Reform of the International Monetary Fund
Peter B. Kenen; CSR No. 29, May 2007
A Maurice R. Greenberg Center for Geoeconomic Studies Report

Nuclear Energy: Balancing Benefits and Risks
Charles D. Ferguson; CSR No. 28, April 2007

Nigeria: Elections and Continuing Challenges
Robert I. Rotberg; CSR No. 27, April 2007
A Center for Preventive Action Report

The Economic Logic of Illegal Immigration
Gordon H. Hanson; CSR No. 26, April 2007
A Maurice R. Greenberg Center for Geoeconomic Studies Report

The United States and the WTO Dispute Settlement System
Robert Z. Lawrence; CSR No. 25, March 2007
A Maurice R. Greenberg Center for Geoeconomic Studies Report

Bolivia on the Brink
Eduardo A. Gamarra; CSR No. 24, February 2007
A Center for Preventive Action Report

After the Surge: The Case for U.S. Military Disengagement from Iraq
Steven N. Simon; CSR No. 23, February 2007

Darfur and Beyond: What Is Needed to Prevent Mass Atrocities
Lee Feinstein; CSR No. 22, January 2007

Avoiding Conflict in the Horn of Africa: U.S. Policy Toward Ethiopia and Eritrea
Terrence Lyons; CSR No. 21, December 2006
A Center for Preventive Action Report

Living with Hugo: U.S. Policy Toward Hugo Chávez's Venezuela
Richard Lapper; CSR No. 20, November 2006
A Center for Preventive Action Report

Reforming U.S. Patent Policy: Getting the Incentives Right
Keith E. Maskus; CSR No. 19, November 2006
A Maurice R. Greenberg Center for Geoeconomic Studies Report

Foreign Investment and National Security: Getting the Balance Right
Alan P. Larson, David M. Marchick; CSR No. 18, July 2006
A Maurice R. Greenberg Center for Geoeconomic Studies Report

Challenges for a Postelection Mexico: Issues for U.S. Policy
Pamela K. Starr; CSR No. 17, June 2006 (web-only release) and November 2006

U.S.-India Nuclear Cooperation: A Strategy for Moving Forward
Michael A. Levi and Charles D. Ferguson; CSR No. 16, June 2006

Generating Momentum for a New Era in U.S.-Turkey Relations
Steven A. Cook and Elizabeth Sherwood-Randall; CSR No. 15, June 2006

Peace in Papua: Widening a Window of Opportunity
Blair A. King; CSR No. 14, March 2006
A Center for Preventive Action Report

Neglected Defense: Mobilizing the Private Sector to Support Homeland Security
Stephen E. Flynn and Daniel B. Prieto; CSR No. 13, March 2006

Afghanistan's Uncertain Transition From Turmoil to Normalcy
Barnett R. Rubin; CSR No. 12, March 2006
A Center for Preventive Action Report

Preventing Catastrophic Nuclear Terrorism
Charles D. Ferguson; CSR No. 11, March 2006

Getting Serious About the Twin Deficits
Menzie D. Chinn; CSR No. 10, September 2005
A Maurice R. Greenberg Center for Geoeconomic Studies Report

Both Sides of the Aisle: A Call for Bipartisan Foreign Policy
Nancy E. Roman; CSR No. 9, September 2005

Forgotten Intervention? What the United States Needs to Do in the Western Balkans
Amelia Branczik and William L. Nash; CSR No. 8, June 2005
A Center for Preventive Action Report

A New Beginning: Strategies for a More Fruitful Dialogue with the Muslim World
Craig Charney and Nicole Yakatan; CSR No. 7, May 2005

Power-Sharing in Iraq
David L. Phillips; CSR No. 6, April 2005
A Center for Preventive Action Report

Giving Meaning to "Never Again": Seeking an Effective Response to the Crisis in Darfur and Beyond
Cheryl O. Igiri and Princeton N. Lyman; CSR No. 5, September 2004

Freedom, Prosperity, and Security: The G8 Partnership with Africa: Sea Island 2004 and Beyond
J. Brian Atwood, Robert S. Browne, and Princeton N. Lyman; CSR No. 4, May 2004

Addressing the HIV/AIDS Pandemic: A U.S. Global AIDS Strategy for the Long Term
Daniel M. Fox and Princeton N. Lyman; CSR No. 3, May 2004
Cosponsored with the Milbank Memorial Fund

Challenges for a Post-Election Philippines
Catharin E. Dalpino; CSR No. 2, May 2004
A Center for Preventive Action Report

Stability, Security, and Sovereignty in the Republic of Georgia
David L. Phillips; CSR No. 1, January 2004
A Center for Preventive Action Report

To purchase a printed copy, call the Brookings Institution Press: 800-537-5487. Council Special Reports are also available to download from the Council's website, CFR.org. For more information, contact publications@cfr.org.